SEND NOODS

50 AMAZING NOODLE RECIPES THAT YOU WANT RIGHT NOW

CHLOE GODOT
ILLUSTRATED BY ALICE POTTER

CASTLE POINT BOOKS
NEW YORK

www.castlepointbooks.com

The Castle Point Books trademark is owned by Castle Point Publishing, LLC.

Castle Point books are published and distributed by St. Martin's Publishing Group.

ISBN 978-1-250-28167-8 (paper over board)
ISBN 978-1-250-28168-5 (ebook)

Illustrations by Alice Potter

Design by Tara Long

Editorial by Monica Sweeney

Our books may be purchased in bulk for promotional, educational, or business use.
Please contact your local bookseller or the Macmillan Corporate and Premium Sales Department
at 1-800-221-7945, extension 5442, or by email at MacmillanSpecialMarkets@macmillan.com.

First Edition: 2022

10 9 8 7 6 5 4 3 2

CONTENTS

1
THE LITTLE BLACK BOOK OF BASICS

The best broths, sauces, and standbys you have ever had

2
HEART WARMERS

Comfort foods that will melt your heart

3 THE BIG SPOON

*Soups you will want to
spoon like you have
never spooned before*

4 TOO FIT to QUIT

*Ogle these health nuts
without stepping foot
in a gym*

5 THE HOTTIES

*Noods that are
fire emoji, fire emoji,
fire emoji*

GET THE NOODS YOU REALLY WANT

THE PHRASE "SEND NOODS" HAS NEVER LOOKED SO GOOD. Why settle for pick-up lines and unsolicited DMs when you can settle into your happy place with something that's truly hot? Complete with the kind of illustrated noodle pics that you'll actually fawn over and 50 delicious recipes, there's a little something here for every appetite. *Send Noods* is the cookbook that will treat you right.

Follow along this look book of gorgeous, satisfying recipes that span every type. Keep up with your go-tos in Chapter One: The Little Black Book of Basics. This section covers all the old favorites that you go back to time after time, like Check You Out Chicken Broth (page 16), Red Flag Red Sauce (page 24), Looking Fresh Pesto (page 28), and How You Doin' Homemade Italian Sausage (page 32).

Move along to Chapter Two, where all your dreams come true with the Heart Warmers. These are the recipes you want to curl up with, like the Mack on this Mac 'n' Cheese (page 38), the Catch Feels Cacio e Pepe (page 41), and the Cuffing Season Tortellini Alfredo (page 42). Feel that special glow of affection in every bite.

Chapter Three: The Big Spoon is exactly what it sounds like—the very best noodle soups that you'll want to hold close, like U Up? Udon (page 60), Swipe Right Ramen (page 64), and Fresh Catch for the Apps Fish Stew (page 75). Fire these up when you're on the prowl for a hot broth that leaves you feeling loved.

It's not every day you want what's good for you. Chapter Four: Too Fit to Quit is the spot where you can lust after some of the healthiest-looking noodle bowls you have ever seen without the flash of panic that comes with joining a spin class. Try the Message in a Bottle Scallops (page 85), Eggplant Emoji Soba Noodles (page 86), and the Mirror Selfie Lettuce Wraps (page 97). Hit these fresh, healthy flavors and never look back.

No book of noods is complete without Chapter Five: The Hotties. They are the ones that leave you hot, bothered, and in need of a cold splash of water—the ones you can't always handle but dream about anyway. Hot in spice and desire, recipes like F*&#boy Fettuccini (page 104), Dreamboat Arrabiata (page115), and Love at First Swipe Pistachio Rigatoni (page 123) promise to leave you breathless.

Make the magic happen with any of these 50 infatuating recipes!

HOW TO DATE THIS COOKBOOK

RECIPE FOR HAPPINESS

Swipe right on some hot dishes that are exactly who they say they are. Will you be wishing, hoping, and wondering how to make these recipes work? *Nope!* What about converting mixed signals and doing confusing mental math to get it just right? *Not today.* Appearing and disappearing text bubbles!? *I. Said. No.* These crystal-clear instructions make their intentions known. Hang on every word and go full clinger if you want to! If something doesn't make sense to you, just wing it, substitute it, or do what you want. No matter what kind of mess you make, these recipes will always love you back.

RECIPE
1. Set timer to forever and a day
2. Add TLC ♡
3. Stir occasionally
4. Keep hot

EMOJIS ARE EVERYTHING

Follow those visual cues! Each recipe features one in a series of smiley faces to indicate the spice level of your dish. The good ol' winky face 😉 is your classic spice level. To call it "mild" isn't doing it justice, because this baby is full of flavor. Step it up to that oh-face 😲 and this recipe is a little bit surprising. It's just a kick of spice to perk you up but always something you can handle. Prepare yourself for the bad boy 😈. Unlike some heartbreakers, this fresh face tells you everything up front. It's hot as hell, and it's sure to blow your mind.

SHIP THESE INGREDIENTS

The ingredients in this book are matches made in heaven. With flavor profiles so perfect you'll think you're being catfished, there is a loving partnership in every bite. But even though they are meant to be together, some of the best relationships started as situationships! If you can't commit to what's listed in the recipe, it's okay to stray to something more convenient. Toss in different veggies if that's what feels right, mix in another meat to get your fill, and know when that box of noodles right in front of your eyes is better than the fancy noodles that play hard to get.

KNOW WHAT'S GOOD FOR YOU

Self-awareness is so important! Sometimes you want something so badly, but it's just not right for you. Maybe homemade spaghetti sounds like your Prince Charming, but you don't have a pasta maker or you have exactly zero patience to make it by hand. That's okay! You don't have to try hard for these babies, and you can always be yourself. Good love sometimes takes work, but it should never hurt.

HAPPY ENDINGS

Get exactly what you are looking for with these 50 incredible recipes. Find your Hotties, show up for your Heart Warmers, and make the most of the time you spend with your Big Spoons. Indulge in all the hot noods you could ever want and none that you don't. Love, lust, and pour your heart out for these satisfying dishes that will keep you coming back for more.

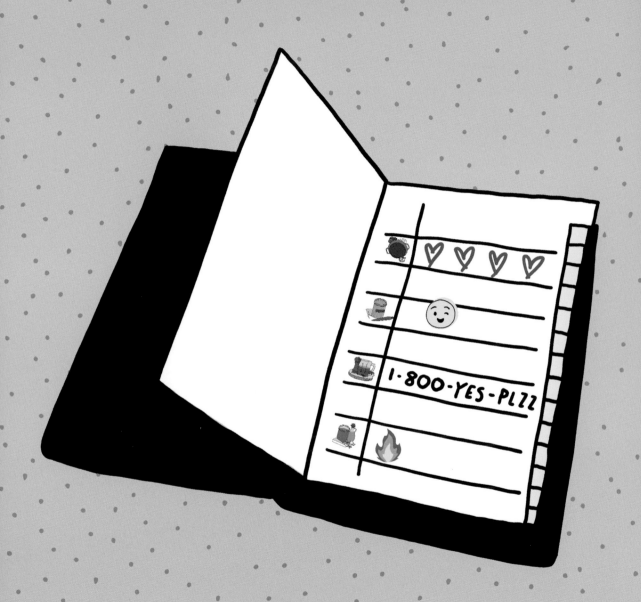

THE LITTLE BLACK BOOK OF BASICS

THE BEST BROTHS, SAUCES, AND STANDBYS YOU HAVE EVER HAD

CHECK YOU OUT CHICKEN BROTH

1 roasted chicken carcass

2 medium yellow onions, peeled

4 stalks celery

2 medium carrots

2 lemons

1 tablespoon whole peppercorns

2 cloves garlic, peeled

1 Place the chicken carcass in a slow cooker. Roughly chop the onions, celery, carrots, and lemons and add them to the slow cooker along with the peppercorns and garlic. Fill the slow cooker with water, making sure to cover the bones or filling up the slow cooker an inch from the top.

2 Place the lid on the slow cooker and cook on low for 8–12 hours.

3 When the broth is finished, carefully remove the ceramic insert from the slow cooker. Strain the broth through a strainer into a large pot. Strain again through a sieve or cheesecloth for clearer broth.

4 Dish out the Check You Out Chicken Broth for all your noodle needs, or allow it to cool and transfer to storage containers. This hot broth will keep for up to a week in the fridge or 2-3 months in the freezer.

🔥 HOT TIP Add 2 tablespoons cayenne to your ingredients list if you're looking to spice things up. Ditch the lemons if you want to mellow things out.

BROODING BEEF BROTH

SPICE LEVEL

1 Preheat the oven to broil. Place the beef bones on a baking sheet. Brown the bones under the broiler for 5 minutes on each side.

2 Transfer the beef bones to a slow cooker. Roughly chop the onions, celery, and carrots and add them to the slow cooker along with the peppercorns, garlic, and bay leaves. Fill the slow cooker with water, making sure to cover the bones or filling up the slow cooker an inch from the top.

3 Place the lid on the slow cooker and cook on low for about 12 hours.

4 When the broth is finished, carefully remove the ceramic insert from the slow cooker. Strain the broth through a strainer and into a large pot. Strain again through a sieve or cheesecloth for clearer broth.

5 Dish out the Brooding Beef Broth for all your noodle needs, or allow it to cool and transfer to storage containers. This hot broth will keep for up to a week in the fridge or 2–3 months in the freezer.

3-4 pounds meaty beef bones

2 medium yellow onions, peeled

4 stalks celery

2 medium carrots

1 tablespoon whole peppercorns

2 cloves garlic, peeled

2 bay leaves

STEAMY STARE VEGGIE BROTH

SERVES 10

2 medium yellow onions, peeled

4 stalks celery

4 medium carrots

2–3 large kale leaves

1 tablespoon whole peppercorns

1 teaspoon sea salt

1 sprig fresh rosemary

2 sprigs fresh thyme

4 cloves garlic, peeled

2 bay leaves

1 Roughly chop the onions, celery, carrots, and kale. Add the veggies to a slow cooker, along with the peppercorns, sea salt, rosemary, thyme, garlic, and bay leaves. Fill the slow cooker with water, making sure to cover the ingredients or filling up the slow cooker an inch from the top.

2 Place the lid on the slow cooker and cook on low for 8–12 hours.

3 When the broth is finished, carefully remove the ceramic insert from the slow cooker. Strain the broth through a strainer and into a large pot. Strain again through a sieve or cheesecloth for clearer broth.

4 Dish out the Steamy Stare Veggie Broth for all your noodle needs, or allow it to cool and transfer to storage containers. This hot broth will keep for up to a week in the fridge or 2–3 months in the freezer.

🔥 **HOT TIP** Add ¼ cup tomato paste or nutritional yeast for that oh-my-umami flavor.

FIND A BASE THAT WILL SWEEP YOU OFF YOUR FEET. This combination style of dashi is easy to prepare but full of depth, and it's flexible enough to make all your umami dishes shine. The Dashing Dashi Broth is that good love that simmers, so get ready for its endless charm.

← SWOON

DASHING DASHI BROTH

1 Cut slits into the dried kelp. Don't you dare rinse off the powdery coating (it adds flavor). In a medium pot over medium-low heat, bring the kelp and water to a boil, about 10 minutes. Skim the surface of the broth with a skimmer periodically.

2 Remove the kelp from the pot. Add the bonito flakes and return the pot to a boil. Reduce the heat to simmer for half a minute and then remove the pot from the heat. Let the broth rest for 10 minutes as the bonito flakes sink to the bottom.

3 Strain the broth through a fine-mesh strainer. Dish out the Dashing Dashi Broth for all your noodle needs, or allow it to cool and transfer to storage containers. This hot broth will keep for up to 5 days in the fridge or 2 weeks in the freezer.

SPICE LEVEL

1 (4 x 4) piece dried kelp

4 cups water

1 cup dried bonito flakes

RED FLAG RED SAUCE

1 (28-ounce) can
Italian plum tomatoes

5 tablespoons butter

1 medium onion, peeled
and cut in half

1 teaspoon red
pepper flakes

Salt and pepper

1 In a saucepan over low heat, combine the tomatoes and their juice, butter, onion, red pepper flakes, and salt and pepper. Break up the tomatoes with forks or mash with a wooden spoon.

2 Cook, uncovered, at a steady simmer for about 45 minutes or until the fat separates. Scoop out the onion or break it up into the sauce for added flavor.

3 Get after this Red Flag Red Sauce or allow it to cool and transfer to storage containers. This hot sauce will keep for up to 5 days in the fridge or 2 weeks in the freezer.

HOT BRO ALFREDO SAUCE

1 In a medium skillet, heat the butter and heavy cream over medium-low heat. When it starts to bubble, lower the heat and let it simmer about 15 minutes, or until it reduces a little.

2 Stir in the Parmesan until well combined, and then add the parsley. Pour this delicious Hot Bro Alfredo Sauce over whatever you can find.

🔥 **HOT TIP** Like your Hot Bros extra cheesy? Replace ½ cup Parmesan with ½ cup cream cheese

 SPICE LEVEL

½ cup butter

2 cups heavy cream

1½ cups freshly grated Parmesan

2 tablespoons chopped fresh parsley

Salt and pepper

LOOKING FRESH PESTO

SERVES 4–6

2 cups fresh basil leaves

2 tablespoons pine nuts

2 large cloves garlic

1/2 cup extra-virgin olive oil

1/2 cup freshly grated Parmesan

1 In a food processor, combine the basil, pine nuts, and garlic and process until finely minced. Slowly drizzle in the olive oil with the food processor still running. When the mixture is smooth, add in the Parmesan and process until just combined.

2 Incorporate the Looking Fresh Pesto into all your favorite dishes.

MY, MY—YOU CLEAN UP NICE. Dress up your favorite recipes with the Looking Fresh Pesto and feel that sense of pride when the one you love is doing you right. Whether you let it show off over an elaborate seafood dish or just let it shine by itself in the noods, this bright and energetic set of flavors will always impress.

I WANT YOU

HEAVEN-SENT
HANDMADE SPAGHETTI

SERVES 3-4

1 Pile the flour on a clean work surface and create a well in the center. Add the eggs, sea salt, and olive oil to the center of the well and begin whisking the eggs gently with a fork. Gradually incorporate the flour, using your hands to bring the dough together to form a ball.

2 Knead the dough about 10 minutes. Sprinkle in a little water or flour if the dough feels dry or wet, respectively. When the dough is smooth, form it into a ball, wrap it in plastic wrap, and let it sit for half an hour at room temperature.

3 Slice the pasta dough into four wedges. Form one wedge into a flat oval. Wrap the other wedges you're not using in plastic wrap so they don't dry out while you work. Send the first oval through the pasta roller on the widest setting (usually setting 1). Feed the dough through the roller once through each setting or until the dough is the right thickness.

4 Dust the dough lightly with flour. Send it through the spaghetti attachment of your pasta maker. Let the spaghetti dry for 30 minutes by draping the noodles over a pasta drying rack, or by curling them into nests on a baking sheet. Repeat steps 3 and 4 with each section of dough.

5 To cook up these heavenly noodles, toss them into boiling salted water for 1 minute.

SPICE LEVEL

2 cups 00 grade or all-purpose flour

3 large eggs

½ teaspoon sea salt

½ tablespoon extra-virgin olive oil

🔥 **HOT TIP** If you're not into toys, you can do all of this by hand. Roll out the dough until it's even in thickness, fold it (dusted) into thirds like a sheet of paper, and cut even ¼-inch ribbons to create fettuccini.

HOW YOU DOIN'
HOMEMADE ITALIAN SAUSAGE

SPICE LEVEL

1 pound ground pork

2 teaspoons fennel seeds, crushed

1/4 teaspoon
red pepper flakes

1 tablespoon salt

1 tablespoon pepper

1 tablespoon
extra-virgin olive oil

1 In a large mixing bowl, use your hands to combine the ground pork, fennel seeds, red pepper flakes, and 1 teaspoon each salt and pepper until the seasonings are evenly distributed.

2 Incorporate the uncooked How You Doin' Homemade Italian Sausage into another recipe, or cook as follows. Shape the sausage into eight patties. In a skillet, heat the olive oil over medium-high heat. When the oil is shimmering, add the sausage patties and cook until browned on both sides and no longer pink in the middle, about 10–12 minutes.

🔥 **HOT TIP** Make this sausage recipe as hot as it gets by adding in extra red pepper flakes.

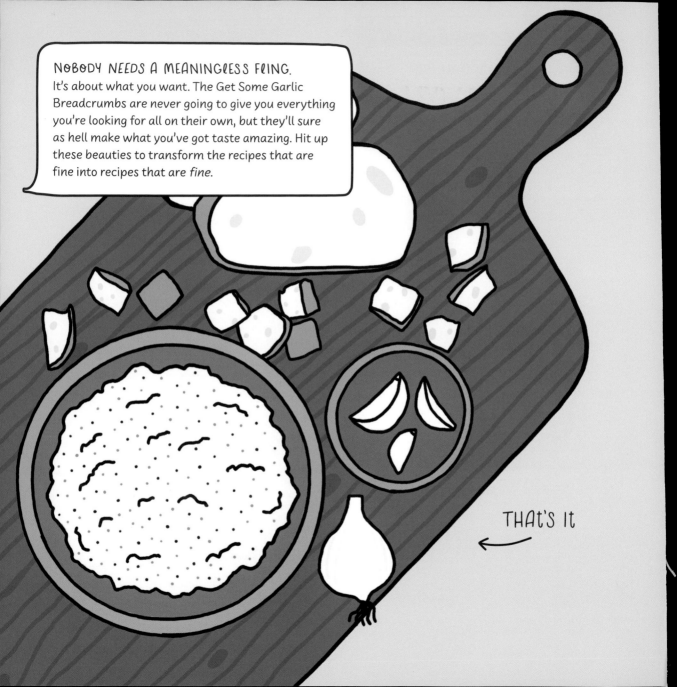

GET SOME GARLIC BREADCRUMBS

SERVES 4–6

SPICE LEVEL

1 In a skillet, heat the butter and olive oil over medium heat. When the butter has melted, stir in the garlic and cook until fragrant. Add the breadcrumbs and cook until browned, about 3–5 minutes. Toss in the lemon zest and parsley.

2 Remove the Get Some Garlic Breadcrumbs from the heat and sprinkle them far and wide.

2 tablespoons butter

2 tablespoons extra-virgin olive oil

1 tablespoon minced garlic

1 cup panko breadcrumbs or dried and smashed bread

1 teaspoon grated lemon zest

2 tablespoons chopped fresh parsley

HEART WARMERS

2.

COMFORT FOODS
THAT WILL
MELT YOUR HEART

MACK ON THIS MAC 'N' CHEESE

2 cups elbow noodles

1½ cups whole milk

3 tablespoons butter, divided

2 tablespoons all-purpose flour

4 ounces Gruyère cheese, shredded

3 ounces extra-sharp cheddar, shredded

¼ teaspoon pepper

1 pinch ground nutmeg

¼ cup panko breadcrumbs

Fresh herbs, for serving

1 Cook the noodles for about 1 minute shy of the package instructions. Drain and set aside.

2 While the noodles are noodling, preheat the oven to 350°F. Warm the milk in a small saucepan over low heat without letting it boil. In a much larger pot, melt 2 tablespoons of the butter over low heat. Gradually whisk in the flour for 2 minutes. Continue to whisk, gradually adding the hot milk from the other pan, and cook, stirring until the sauce thickens slightly.

3 Remove the pot from the heat and mix in the Gruyère, cheddar, pepper, nutmeg, and noodles.

4 To get the crunch of your dreams, combine 1 tablespoon butter and the breadcrumbs in a small saucepan over medium heat. When the butter is absorbed, let the breadcrumbs toast just a bit before removing them from the heat.

5 Pour the mac into a baking dish and scatter the breadcrumbs over the top. Bake it for 10–15 minutes, or until the top is bubbling and slightly browned. Remove it from the oven and give yourself a good helping. Garnish your mac with parsley or thyme to fancy things up.

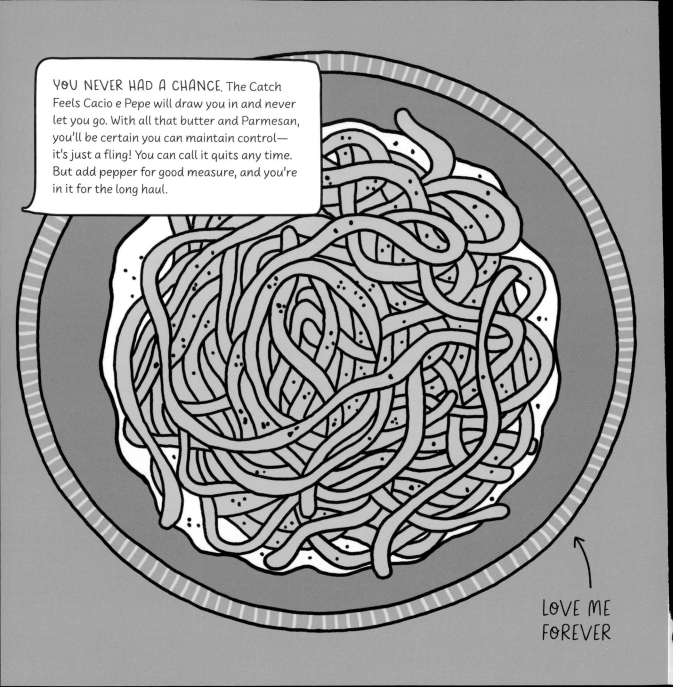

CATCH FEELS CACIO E PEPE

1 Cook the bucatini noodles about 1 minute shy of the package instructions. Drain, reserving 1 cup of the pasta water, and set aside.

2 In a saucepan, melt 2 tablespoons of the butter. Add the pepper and toast about 1 minute. Add ½ cup of the pasta water to the pan and bring to a simmer. Stir in the bucatini and the rest of the butter. Reduce the heat and mix in the Parmesan.

3 Remove the pan from the heat. Toss in the Pecorino until the pasta is coated and glossy. Add a little more of the reserved pasta water if the bucatini is too dry. It's okay, now go Catch Feels Cacio e Pepe.

 SPICE LEVEL

6 ounces bucatini noodles

3 tablespoons butter, divided

1 teaspoon freshly ground black pepper

3/4 cup freshly grated Parmesan

1/3 cup freshly grated Pecorino

CUFFING SEASON
TORTELLINI ALFREDO

SPICE LEVEL

½ (9-ounce) package tortellini noodles

1½ cups Hot Bro Alfredo Sauce (page 27)

½ cup sundried tomatoes in oil

½ teaspoon sundried tomato oil

1–2 cloves garlic, minced

Salt and pepper

Freshly grated Parmesan

1 Cook the tortellini about 1 minute shy of the package instructions. Drain and set aside.

2 In a saucepan, heat the Hot Bro Alfredo Sauce over medium heat to warm through.

3 Slice the sundried tomatoes into strips. In a small skillet, heat the sundried tomato oil. Sauté the sundried tomatoes and garlic until lightly browned. Remove from the heat and set aside.

4 Stir the cooked tortellini and garlicky sundried tomatoes into the pot of alfredo. Dish out this sizzler with even more cheese!

FRIENDZONE FIDEUÀ

SERVES 2

1 Preheat the oven to 375°F. Scatter the fideo noodles onto a baking sheet, coat with 2 tablespoons of the olive oil. Bake 8–10 minutes until lightly browned. Remove from the oven and set aside.

2 Increase the oven temperature to 450°F. In a medium saucepan, simmer the veggie broth over medium heat. In a small bowl, mash the garlic, ⅛ teaspoon salt, and the parsley to make a paste. Stir in ½ tablespoon of the olive oil and set the mixture aside.

3 In a wide skillet, heat the remaining 2 tablespoons olive oil over high heat. When the oil is shimmering, add the squid and cook until it is opaque, about 1–2 minutes. Toss in the fideo noodles.

4 Add the garlic paste, sofrito, onion powder, paprika, ¼ teaspoon salt, and ¼ teaspoon pepper. Pour in 3 cups of the veggie broth and bring it to a boil, shaking the pan but not stirring the contents. Reduce the heat to medium and let simmer, about 10 minutes, or until some of the broth is absorbed. Add 1 cup more veggie broth if the noodles aren't free-floating, and cook for another 10 minutes, or until there's just a little broth resting on the surface.

5 Fold in the shrimp and add the mussels and peas. Transfer the pan to the oven and cook until the shrimp is opaque, the mussels have opened, and the broth has absorbed, about 5–7 minutes.

6 Remove the pan from the oven and serve up the good stuff! Transfer the Friendzone Fideuà to bowls and garnish with the aioli and a spritz of lemon.

 SPICE LEVEL

4 ounces fideo noodles

4½ tablespoons extra-virgin olive oil, divided

4 cups Steamy Stare Veggie Broth (page 20)

1 clove garlic, peeled

⅛ teaspoon plus ½ teaspoon kosher salt

6 tablespoons chopped fresh parsley

½ cup squid rings

¼ cup sofrito

½ teaspoon onion powder

½ teaspoon smoked paprika

Salt and pepper

½ pound mussels

8 medium shrimp, peeled and deveined

¼ cup frozen peas, thawed

2 tablespoons aioli

2 lemon wedges

BE MY VALENTINE VERMICELLI

SERVES 2

1 tablespoon
light soy sauce

1 tablespoon rice wine
vinegar

3/4 teaspoon sugar

1 tablespoon
grapeseed oil

1 clove garlic, minced

1/2 red chili, minced

2 ounces dried vermicelli
noodles

1 cup shredded
green cabbage

3/4 cup shredded carrot

3/4 cup bean sprouts

1 scallion, chopped

1/4 cup chopped
fresh cilantro

1 tablespoon fried shallots

1 In a small bowl, whisk together the soy sauce, rice wine vinegar, sugar, grapeseed oil, garlic, and red chili. Set aside.

2 Cook the vermicelli noodles according to the package instructions. Drain the noodles and pat them dry with a towel. Toss the vermicelli with the cabbage, carrot, bean sprouts, scallion, and cilantro. Add the dressing and toss until well combined.

3 Get to the good stuff! Serve the Be My Valentine Vermicelli in bowls and garnish with fried shallots.

NICE GUY SHRIMP PAD THAI

1 Cook the rice noodles about 1 minute shy of the package instructions. Drain and set aside.

2 In a small bowl, whisk together the tamari, fish sauce, vinegar, honey, and red pepper flakes.

3 In a large skillet, heat the peanut oil over medium heat. When the oil is shimmering, add the shrimp and cook until it is opaque, about 2–3 minutes. Stir in the butter, garlic, and a pinch of pepper and cook for another minute or two.

4 Stir in the noodles and sauce. Push the contents of the pan to one side and add the egg. Allow it to cook for 1 minute before scrambling and incorporating into the noodles.

5 Get after it! Transfer the noodles into serving bowls and top with the scallion, peanuts, and Thai basil. Spritz this Nice Guy Pad Thai with a little lime.

 SPICE LEVEL

4 ounces rice noodles

2 tablespoons tamari

1 tablespoon fish sauce

1 tablespoon white vinegar

1 1/2 tablespoons honey

1/2 teaspoon red pepper flakes

1/2 tablespoon peanut oil

1/2 pound jumbo shrimp, peeled and deveined

1 1/2 tablespoons butter

2 cloves garlic, minced

Pepper

1 egg, beaten

1 scallion, chopped

1/4 cup chopped roasted peanuts

4–6 fresh Thai basil leaves

2 lime wedges

WON'T CLAM UP
SPAGHETTI & CLAMS

1 (6.5-ounce) can minced clams

1/4 cup extra-virgin olive oil

6 cloves garlic, minced

1/2 teaspoon red pepper flakes

2 cups canned whole tomatoes, drained and chopped

1/2 batch Heaven-Sent Handmade Spaghetti (page 31) or 4 ounces dry spaghetti

2 tablespoons chopped fresh parsley

Salt and pepper

Freshly grated Parmesan

1 Drain the clams, reserving 1/2 cup of their juice. In a large skillet, heat the olive oil over medium-low heat. When the oil is shimmering, add the garlic and cook until fragrant, about 2–3 minutes. Stir in the red pepper flakes, followed by the reserved clam juice and the tomatoes. When it begins to boil, cover the pan, reduce the heat, and simmer for about 15 minutes.

2 Cook the Heaven-Sent Homemade Spaghetti in salted boiling water for 1 minute, or prepare dry spaghetti according to the package instructions. Drain and set aside.

3 Stir the clams and parsley into the sauce. Toss in the spaghetti until well combined. Transfer the Won't Clam Up Spaghetti & Clams to serving bowls and sprinkle salt, pepper, and Parmesan with abandon.

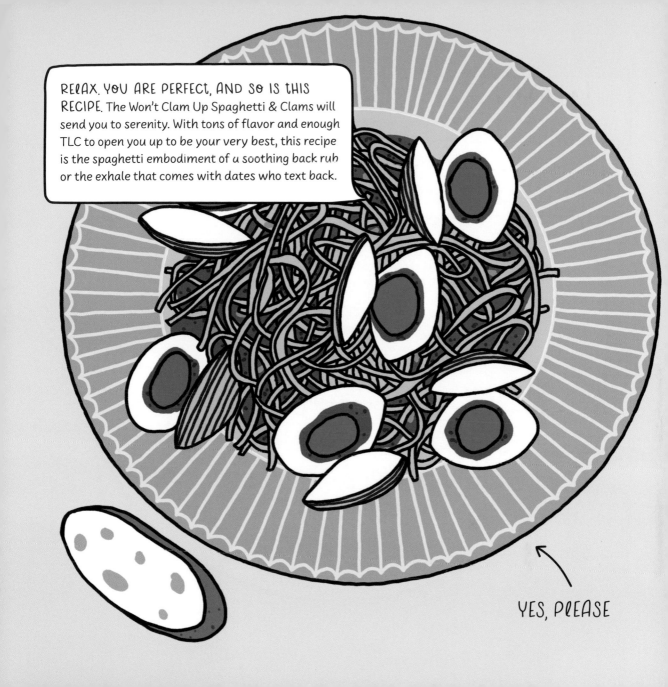

BEEFCAKE BEEF STROGANOFF

1 Cook the egg noodles about 1 minute shy of the package instructions. Drain and set aside.

2 In a large skillet, melt the butter over medium heat. Stir in the mushrooms and onion and cook for 3–5 minutes. Sprinkle with salt and pepper. Add the ground beef and cook until it begins to brown, about 3–5 minutes. Stir in the garlic and thyme, and then the flour, and cook, stirring, for about 1 minute.

3 Add the wine, deglazing the pan before stirring in the beef broth, Worcestershire, mustard, and egg noodles. Bring everything to a boil, and then reduce the heat and let it simmer, about 8–10 minutes. Stir in the yogurt before removing the pan from the heat. Set the table with this Beefcake Beef Stroganoff, and sprinkle it with parsley before devouring.

 SPICE LEVEL

4 ounces egg noodles

1 tablespoon butter

6 ounces cremini mushrooms, sliced

1/4 medium sweet onion, diced

Salt and pepper

1/2 pound ground beef

1 clove garlic, minced

1/4 teaspoon dried thyme

1 1/2 tablespoons all-purpose flour

2 tablespoons dry white wine

2 cups Brooding Beef Broth (page 19)

1 tablespoon Worcestershire sauce

1/2 tablespoon Dijon mustard

1/4 cup Greek yogurt

1 tablespoon chopped fresh parsley

LIGHTS OUT LOBSTER TAGLIATELLE

SERVES 2

2 cups dry white wine

3–4 sprigs fresh thyme

2 (5-ounce) lobster tails

4 ounces tagliatelle noodles

1 tablespoon extra-virgin olive oil

1 medium shallot, finely chopped

2 cloves garlic, minced

Salt and pepper

1 cup heavy cream

2 tablespoons butter

Grated zest of 1 lemon

1/3 cup freshly grated Parmesan

1 tablespoon lemon juice

2–3 fresh basil leaves, ripped

2 lemon wedges

1 In a medium saucepan, combine the wine and thyme and bring to a boil. Add the lobster tails and reduce the heat to a simmer. Cover the saucepan, cooking until the lobster shells turn red and curl, about 5–6 minutes. Remove the lobster tails from the pan and cut the underside of the bellies down the center to remove the meat. Chop the meat into large chunks and set aside.

2 Cook the tagliatelle about 1 minute shy of the package instructions. Drain, reserving 1 cup of the pasta water, and set aside.

3 In a large skillet, heat the olive oil over medium heat. When the oil is shimmering, add the shallot, garlic, and a pinch of salt and pepper. Cook, stirring until fragrant, about 1–2 minutes. Pour in the heavy cream and increase the heat to a simmer. When the cream begins to bubble gently, reduce the heat and incorporate the butter, lemon zest, Parmesan, and a sprinkling of salt. When the mixture is well-combined, stir in ¼ cup of the pasta water and the lemon juice. Add the lobster meat and cook, stirring continuously, about 1 minute.

4 Stir in the tagliatelle to coat. If the sauce is too thick, add more pasta water until the tagliatelle is glossy. Pretty up the Lights Out Lobster Tagliatelle with a smattering of ripped basil and lemon wedges when serving.

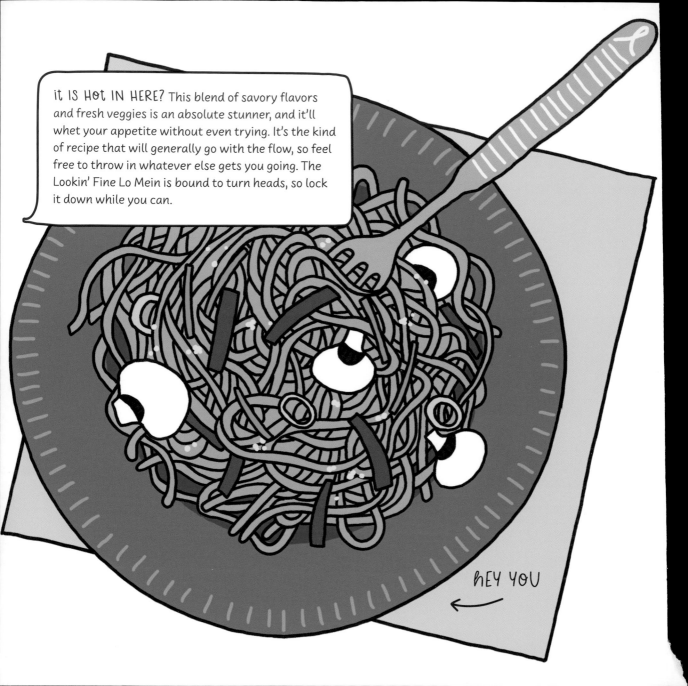

LOOKIN' FINE LO MEIN

1 In a small bowl, whisk together the soy sauces, ½ teaspoon sesame oil, and the sugar.

2 Cook the egg noodles about 1 minute shy of the package instructions. Drrain and set aside.

3 In a large wok or skillet, heat ½ tablespoon sesame oil. Add the white parts of the scallion and all of the vegetables to the wok to stir fry, about 5 minutes. Stir in the mirin to deglaze the pan before adding the cooked noodles. Toss the noodles and gradually add in the sauce until the noodles are dressed to your liking.

4 Time to dish it out! Transfer the Lookin' Fine Lo Mein to bowls and garnish with the rest of the scallion.

 SPICE LEVEL

1 tablespoon dark soy sauce

1/2 tablespoon light soy sauce

1/2 teaspoon plus 1/2 tablespoon sesame oil, divided

1/2 teaspoon sugar

4 ounces Hong Kong egg noodles

1 scallion, chopped

1/2 cup julienned carrots

1/2 cup julienned red bell pepper

1/2 cup julienned snow peas

1/2 cup sliced mushrooms

1/2 cup baby corn

1 tablespoon mirin

THE BIG SPOON

3

SOUPS YOU WILL WANT TO SPOON LIKE YOU HAVE NEVER SPOONED BEFORE

U UP? UDON

SERVES 2

2 cups Dashing Dashi Broth (page 23)

2½ teaspoons sugar, divided

1 tablespoon mirin or sake

2 tablespoons soy sauce, divided

4 ounces udon noodles

1 tablespoon vegetable oil

3 scallions, sliced, divided

½ pound thinly sliced beef chuck

6 slices narutomaki

½ medium carrot, shredded

Shichimi togarashi

1 In a small saucepan, combine the dashi broth, 1 teaspoon of the sugar, the mirin, and 1 tablespoon soy sauce, and bring to a boil. Cover and reduce the heat to low while you cook the rest.

2 Cook the udon noodles about 1 minute shy of the package instructions. Drain and set aside.

3 In a large frying pan, heat the vegetable oil and sauté the white part of the scallions. Add the beef to the pan and sear it on all sides until browned. Add ½ tablespoon sugar and 1 tablespoon soy sauce to caramelize the beef. Immediately remove from the heat.

4 Put a portion of noodles in a soup bowl. Ladle the broth over the noodles and top the bowl with the beef, narutomaki, the green parts of the scallions, carrot, and a sprinkle of togarashi. Save the rest for later or be a good sharer.

🔥 **HOT TIP** Narutomaki is the pop-of-pink fish cake you see adorning many Japanese noodle dishes, but if it's out of your league (or not at your local store), you can swap in more veggies or a hard-boiled egg.

WHEN IT'S LATE AND YOU NEED AN ABSOLUTE SNACK, SET YOUR SIGHTS ON U UP? UDON. This steamy bowl of noods—perfected by the Dashing Dashi Broth (page 23)—will arouse your senses and fulfill your yearnings for something hearty. Take this hot soup back to bed for a warming wind-down if that's your thing. Or hey, you can just go wild at your kitchen table.

TAKE ME TO BED

PHO, YES. This classic approach to chicken pho is eager to please and won't keep you waiting and agonizing—you can whip it up in less than 15 minutes. While you can add extra veggies or spices to liven this bowl up, there's really no need. Some fleeting romances are better than others, and this one will have you lost in reverie for bowls of pho to come.

OH YES!

SEX IS COOL,
BUT HAVE YOU TRIED MY PHO?

1 Cook the rice noodles about 1 minute shy of the package instructions. Drain and set aside.

2 In a large pot, heat 1 tablespoon olive oil over medium heat. Season the chicken with salt and pepper and cook for 2–3 minutes or until golden. Remove the chicken from the pot and set it aside.

3 Sauté the garlic and ginger in 1 tablespoon olive oil for 1–2 minutes or until aromatic. Stir in the chicken broth, hoisin, and fish sauce, and bring to a boil. Reduce the heat and let it simmer for 10 minutes.

4 Get spooning! Place each helping of noodles into a serving bowl. Ladle the broth over the noodles and top the bowls with the chicken, onion, bean sprouts, cilantro, and mint. Serve with lime wedges and a drizzle of hot sauce, if you like.

 SPICE LEVEL

4 ounces rice noodles

2 tablespoons extra-virgin olive oil, divided

1/2 pound boneless, skinless chicken thighs, cubed

Salt and pepper

1–2 cloves garlic, minced

1/2 tablespoon minced ginger

3 cups chicken broth

1 tablespoon hoisin sauce

1/2 tablespoon fish sauce

1 onion, thinly sliced

1 cup bean sprouts

1/4 cup chopped fresh cilantro

1/4 cup fresh mint leaves

1 red chili, thinly sliced

1 lime, cut into wedges

Hot sauce (optional)

SWIPE RIGHT RAMEN

SPICE LEVEL

4 cremini mushrooms, sliced

1 medium carrot, sliced

1 tablespoon
extra-virgin olive oil

1–2 cloves garlic, minced

2 cups Steamy Stare Veggie
Broth (page 20)

1 teaspoon minced ginger

1/2 tablespoon soy sauce

1/2 tablespoon sesame oil

1/2 tablespoon rice wine
vinegar

2 (3-ounce) packages
ramen noodles

4–6 shrimp,
peeled and deveined

1/2 cup snow peas

1/2 small zucchini, spiralized

1 scallion, sliced

1/4 watermelon radish,
thinly sliced

2 soft-boiled eggs, halved

1 teaspoon sesame seeds

Hot sauce (optional)

1 In a medium pot, sauté the mushrooms and carrot in olive oil for 5 minutes, or until they begin to soften. Add the garlic and cook, stirring until aromatic. Add the vegetable broth, ginger, soy sauce, sesame oil, and rice wine vinegar. Let everything come to a boil.

2 Place the noodles into the pot. Add the shrimp and the snow peas. (If you want to invite more veggies to this party, add them now.) Cover and continue to boil for 3 minutes, or until the noodles are broken up and the shrimp is pink.

3 Time to dish it out! Top your ramen bowl with zoodles, scallion, radish, soft-boiled egg, sesame seeds, and a drizzle of hot sauce if you want to heat things up. Save the rest for round two.

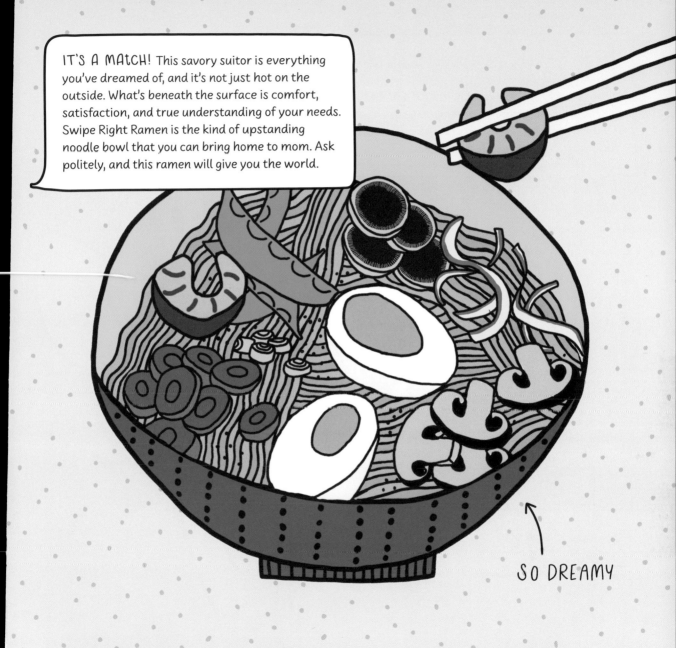

THE OG COMFORT SOUP DESERVES AN OG PICKUP LINE. Come Here Often? Chicken Noodle Soup is highly satisfying, highly spoonable, and you better believe it'll cure you of your dry spell. (Well, for noods.) Don't be shy and give the broth your best shot—it's what takes this classic home.

SO STEAMY

COME HERE OFTEN?
CHICKEN NOODLE SOUP

1 Cook the egg noodles about 1 minute shy of the package instructions. Drain and set aside.

2 In a large saucepan, heat the olive oil over medium-high heat. When the oil is shimmering, add the carrot, celery, and onion. Sauté the vegetables for several minutes, until softened. Add the garlic and continue to cook, about 1 minute.

3 Add the chicken broth, bay leaf, thyme, oregano, and a sprinkle of salt and pepper. Bring the pot to a boil, about 5 minutes, before adding the chicken and parsley. Cook until the chicken is warm.

4 Transfer the egg noodles to serving bowls and ladle this baby up!

🔥 **HOT TIP** You can make shredded chicken by poaching or slow-cooking chicken thighs or breasts and then tearing the meat apart with two forks. If you're in for a quickie, just use precooked rotisserie chicken for all your shredded chicken needs.

SPICE LEVEL

1 cup wide egg noodles

2 tablespoons extra-virgin olive oil

1 medium carrot, sliced

1 stalk celery, sliced

1 small yellow onion, diced

2 cloves garlic, minced

2 cups Check You Out Chicken Broth (page 16)

1 bay leaf

1/2 teaspoon dried thyme

1/2 teaspoon dried oregano

Salt and pepper

1 cup shredded cooked chicken

1 tablespoon chopped fresh parsley

CUDDLE UP CURRY NOODLES

4 ounces rice noodles

2 tablespoons vegetable oil

1 shallot, chopped

2 cloves garlic, chopped

1 tablespoon minced lemongrass

1 tablespoon minced ginger

1 tablespoon Thai yellow curry paste

1 tablespoon curry powder

1/2 teaspoon hot chili paste

1 (14-ounce) can coconut milk, divided

2 1/2 cups chicken broth

1 1/4 tablespoons fish sauce

1 teaspoons sugar

1 large sweet potato, peeled and cubed

1 1/2 cups snow peas

1 cup shredded chicken

1/4 cup thinly sliced red onion

1 scallion, sliced

2 Thai chilies, sliced

1 lime, cut into wedges

1 Cook the rice noodles about 1 minute shy of the package instructions. Drain and set aside.

2 In a large saucepan, heat the vegetable oil over medium heat. When the oil is shimmering, cook the shallots, garlic, lemongrass, and ginger until fragrant, about 1 minute. Reduce the heat and blend in the curry paste, curry powder, and chili paste. Stir in a 1/2 cup of the coconut milk and simmer to let the flavors combine, about 2 minutes. Pour in the rest of the coconut milk, the chicken broth, fish sauce, and sugar and bring the mixture to a boil.

3 Add the sweet potato and cook over medium-high heat, about 10 minutes. Drop in the snow peas and the chicken and simmer, about 7 minutes until the sweet potato is tender.

4 Get noodling! Transfer the rice noodles to a serving bowls, dish up steamy portions of the soup, and top with red onion, scallions, chilies, and a spritz of lime.

COMPLEX ON THE OUTSIDE BUT WARM, LOVING, AND GENEROUS ON THE INSIDE, CUDDLE UP CURRY NOODLES IS THE DISH THAT KEEPS ON GIVING. When you put in the work to woo this heartthrob, it will show you it cares with endless flavor and nourishment that you never thought you deserved.

SO CUDDLY

SPOON ME SAUSAGE SOUP

SERVES 2

1 Cook the rice noodles about 1 minute shy of the package instructions. Drain and set aside.

2 In a large saucepan, heat the olive oil over medium heat. When the oil is shimmering, cook the sausage until browned, about 8–10 minutes.

3 Pour in the chicken broth and bring the mixture to a boil, then reduce the heat to simmer, about 8 minutes. Fold in the mustard greens, scallions, red pepper flakes, soy sauce, and fish sauce and cook until the greens have wilted and the flavors have combined, about 5 minutes.

4 Toss those rice noodles into your bowl and ladle up the soup!

 SPICE LEVEL

4 ounces wide rice noodles

1/2 portion (1/2 pound) How You Doin' Homemade Italian Sausage (page 32)

1 tablespoon extra-virgin olive oil

4 cups Check You Out Chicken Broth (page 16)

4 cups torn mustard greens

4 scallions, thinly sliced

1/4 teaspoon red pepper flakes

2 tablespoons soy sauce

1 teaspoon fish sauce

NEVER LEFT ON READ
VEGGIE BRODO

SPICE LEVEL

4 ounces capellini noodles

4 cups Steamy Stare
Veggie Broth (page 20)

1½ ounces thinly sliced
prosciutto, chopped

¼ cup dried
porcini mushrooms

2 cloves garlic, chopped

4 spears asparagus,
cut into pieces

½ cup fiddleheads

Salt and pepper

¼ cup thinly sliced
button mushrooms

½ tablespoon lemon juice

1 cup pea shoots

1 Cook the capellini noodles about 1 minute shy of the package instructions. Drain and set aside.

2 In a large saucepan, bring the veggie broth to a boil. Reduce the heat to a simmer and add in the prosciutto, porcini mushrooms, and garlic to infuse the broth, about 15 minutes. Strain the broth through a fine-mesh strainer and return to the saucepan.

3 Add the asparagus and fiddleheads, cooking until they turn bright green, about 2–3 minutes. Season with salt and pepper. Remove the soup from the heat and add in the button mushrooms.

4 In a small bowl, whisk the lemon juice and ¼ teaspoon each of salt and pepper and use it to dress the pea shoots.

5 Serve up the good stuff! Ladle the soup into bowls over the capellini and top with the lemony pea shoots before getting into it.

FRESH CATCH FOR THE APPS
FISH STEW

SERVES 2

1 Cook the udon noodles about 1 minute shy of the package instructions. Drain and set aside.

2 In a large pot, bring the dashi broth and soy sauce to a heavy simmer.

3 In a skillet, heat the olive oil over medium heat. Cut the cod into 2 filets and season with salt and pepper. When the oil is shimmering, sear the cod on one side until the fish is no longer translucent and has browned on the bottom, about 5 minutes. Remove from the heat.

4 Add the orange peels to the broth and let steep, about 2 minutes. Remove the peels from the pot and add the spring onions, another 2 minutes. Add the snap peas, Swiss chard, and dandelion greens. When the greens have brightened, ladle them into bowls over the udon.

5 Place the fish on top of the bowls, drizzle with sesame oil, and devour.

 SPICE LEVEL

4 ounces udon noodles

4 cups Dashing Dashi Broth (page 23)

1 tablespoon soy sauce

2 tablespoons extra-virgin olive oil

4 ounces cod filet

Salt and pepper

2 orange peels

4 spring onion bulbs, quartered

1/4 cup snap peas, trimmed

1/2 cup chopped Swiss chard

1/2 cup chopped dandelion greens

1 tablespoon sesame oil

TOO GOOD TO GHOST
GREEN CURRY SOUP

SERVES 2

4 ounces rice noodles

1 tablespoon coconut oil

1/4 cup thinly sliced shallot

1 tablespoon minced ginger

1 clove garlic, minced

1 1/2 tablespoons green curry paste

1 (14-ounce) can coconut milk

1 1/2 cups Check You Out Chicken Broth (page 16)

1 tablespoon tamari

1/2 lemongrass stalk, trimmed

1/2 teaspoon agave syrup

1/2 Thai chili, sliced

Salt and pepper

1 cup shredded cooked chicken

2 sprigs fresh mint

4 lime wedges

1 Cook the rice noodles about 1 minute shy of the package instructions. Drain and set aside.

2 In a skillet, heat the coconut oil over medium heat. When the oil is shimmering, sauté the shallot, ginger, and garlic until fragrant, about 2 minutes. Stir in the curry paste and cook for another minute. Add in the coconut milk, chicken broth, tamari, lemongrass, agave, Thai chili, and a dash of salt and pepper. Bring the mixture to a boil. Reduce the heat, add the chicken, and let simmer until the chicken is warmed, about 5 minutes.

3 Transfer the rice noodles to bowls, ladle out the soup, and garnish with the mint and lime before indulging.

WIFE ME VEGAN MINESTRONE

1 In a large pot, heat the olive oil over medium heat. When the oil is shimmering, sauté the onion and garlic until fragrant, about 2 minutes. Add the celery, carrots, and green beans. Sprinkle with a dash of salt and pepper and cook for 2–3 minutes, or until the veggies have brightened.

2 Stir in the zucchini, crushed tomatoes, veggie broth, basil, and oregano. Bring the mixture to a gentle boil.

3 Reduce the heat to a simmer and add the white beans and the fusilli noodles, cooking for about 10 minutes. Stir in the spinach and cook another 5 minutes. Transfer to bowls and overdo it with Parmesan.

🔥 **HOT TIP** Add a teaspoon of nutritional yeast, coconut aminos, or tamari for that oh-my-umami flavor.

 SPICE LEVEL

2 tablespoons extra-virgin olive oil

1/2 cup diced onion

1 clove garlic, minced

1 stalk celery, sliced

1 medium carrot, sliced

1/2 cup chopped green beans

Salt and pepper

1/2 small zucchini, sliced

1 cup crushed tomatoes

2 cups Steamy Stare Veggie Broth (page 20)

1 teaspoon dried basil

1 teaspoon dried oregano

1/4 cup white beans, drained and rinsed

1/2 cup fusilli noodles

1/2 cup spinach

Freshly grated Parmesan

TOO FIT to QUIT

OGLE THESE
HEALTH NUTS
WITHOUT STEPPING
FOOT IN A GYM

NICE FLEX STEAK & PESTO ZOODLES

SERVES 2

8 ounces flank steak

Salt and pepper

2 medium zucchinis, spiralized

1 tablespoon extra-virgin olive oil

1 handful cherry tomatoes

1–2 tablespoons Looking Fresh Pesto (page 28)

Freshly grated Parmesan

Crushed red pepper flakes

Toasted pine nuts

1 Season the flank steak with salt and pepper (like you mean it), and let it sit for about an hour to tenderize the meat. Preheat the broiler, and then place the steak on a baking sheet on the top rack, or about 6 inches away. Broil for 3–5 minutes on each side, or until the steak has reached 125°F, for medium-rare. Remove the steak from the oven and allow it to rest on a cutting board.

2 In a skillet, heat the olive oil over medium-low heat. When the oil is shimmering, cook the zoodles and cherry tomatoes for 2 minutes while stirring continuously, lightly sprinkling in more salt and pepper. Add the pesto and toss the zoodles until well coated.

3 Dish out those pesto zoodles! Slice the steak into thin strips and lay them on top. Sprinkle the dish with the Parmesan, red pepper flakes, and pine nuts to blow your own mind.

CRAVING SOMETHING STEAMY THAT'S ACTUALLY GOOD FOR YOU? This health nut will satisfy your need for nutrients but won't wake you up for a 5K on a holiday. Make good use of the Looking Fresh Pesto (page 28), or just grab the jarred kind if you prefer a quickie. With pesto-lathered zoodles, a burst of cherry tomato, and savory steak, you'll get to flex all of the best flavors of pesto pasta without anyone telling you to watch your carbs.

LOOKIN' FIT!

ARE YOU A BIG-CITY WORKAHOLIC WHO'S BEEN DRAGGED BACK TO HER SALTY SEASIDE HOMETOWN DECADES LATER FOR AN UNLIKELY REASON? Great, because this recipe has all the flavors of a coastal town in autumn and tastes so perfect it might just be made for TV. With lemony sea scallops and thyme-flecked squash noodles, the Message in a Bottle Scallops are one romance you won't forget.

SO GOOD

MESSAGE IN A BOTTLE
SCALLOPS

1 Preheat the oven to 400°F. Line a baking sheet with parchment paper or foil. Transfer the squash ribbons to the baking sheet and toss with the coconut oil, salt, and thyme until well coated. Roast the noodles for 10 minutes, and then broil for 1–2 minutes to lightly brown. Snag the baking sheet out of the oven when finished.

2 While the squash is baking, whisk together the lemon juice, ginger, and a sprinkle of salt and pepper in a bowl. Add the scallops to the bowl and let them marinate for 10 minutes.

3 In a frying pan, heat the olive oil over high heat. When the oil is shimmering, add the scallops and some of the marinade to the pan. Sauté the scallops for 4 minutes on each side, or until lightly browned.

4 Place a helping of butternut squash ribbons on a plate and top it with a serving of scallops. Sprinkle with some of the lemon zest. Ahoy, indeed.

SPICE LEVEL

2 cups butternut squash ribbons

1 tablespoon coconut oil, melted

1 teaspoon salt

2 sprigs fresh thyme

2 tablespoons extra-virgin olive oil

1 tablespoon minced ginger

Salt and pepper

Grated zest and juice of 1 lemon, divided

8 sea scallops

EGGPLANT EMOJI
SOBA NOODLES

SPICE LEVEL

1 medium
Japanese eggplant

1/4 teaspoon salt

4 ounces green beans,
cut into bite-size pieces

1 teaspoon plus
1 1/2 tablespoons sesame oil,
divided

4 ounces soba noodles

1 1/2 tablespoons
miso paste

1 tablespoon brown sugar

1 tablespoon
red wine vinegar

1 tablespoon soy sauce

1 clove garlic, minced

1 teaspoon minced ginger

1 teaspoon sesame seeds

1 Preheat the grill to medium heat. Cut the eggplant into 1/4-inch-thick slices, sprinkle them with salt, and rest on paper towels for 15 minutes.

2 Lay out a double layer of foil, about 2 feet in length. Place the green beans on one side and coat them with 1 teaspoon of the sesame oil. Fold up the foil into a packet and grill for about 10 minutes, turning halfway through. Remove from the heat and set aside.

3 Cook the soba noodles according to the package instructions. Drain and set aside.

4 In a small bowl, whisk together the miso paste, brown sugar, red wine vinegar, soy sauce, garlic, ginger, and remaining 1 1/2 tablespoons sesame oil. Go back to your eggplant and press out any excess liquid on the paper towels. Generously coat the eggplant in the marinade and grill 8–10 minutes, or until they are crisp, turning halfway through.

5 Toss it all together in bowls and sprinkle with the sesame seeds.

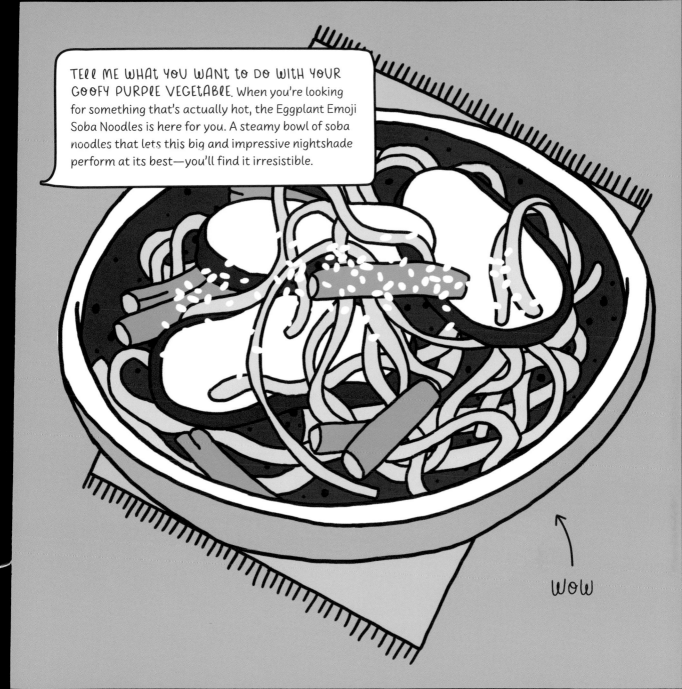

JUST MY TYPE SHRIMP & ZOODLES

1 In a skillet, heat the olive oil over medium-low heat. When the oil is shimmering, sauté the garlic, shrimp, zoodles, and sundried tomatoes. Stir continuously, lightly sprinkling in salt, pepper, and red pepper flakes.

2 Get after it. Transfer to plates and sprinkle the dish with the Parmesan and more red pepper flakes.

SPICE LEVEL

1 tablespoon
extra-virgin olive oil

1 tablespoon minced garlic

1/2 pound shrimp,
peeled and deveined

2 medium zucchinis,
spiralized

3–4 sundried tomatoes
in oil, sliced

Salt and pepper

Red pepper flakes

1 tablespoon freshly grated
Parmesan

PERFECT TEN PRIMAVERA

4 ounces bowtie noodles

1 tablespoon
extra-virgin olive oil

4 spears asparagus,
cut into 2-inch pieces

1/2 yellow bell pepper,
cut into 1-inch pieces

1/2 cup small broccoli florets

1/2 small zucchini, chopped

Salt and pepper

2 tablespoons butter

1/2 shallot, minced

1 clove garlic, minced

Grated zest of 1/2 lemon

1 cup Steamy Stare Veggie
Broth (page 20)

1/2 cup heavy cream

3 tablespoons lemon juice,
divided

1/4 cup frozen peas, thawed

2 tablespoons freshly
grated Parmesan

1/2 cup halved cherry
tomatoes

1 tablespoon chopped
fresh basil

1 Cook the bowtie noodles about 1 minute shy of the package
instructions. Drain and set aside.

2 In a large skillet, heat the olive oil over medium-high heat. When
the oil is shimmering, sauté the asparagus, bell peppers and
broccoli until they brighten, about 3 minutes. Add the zucchini,
cooking until it is tender-crisp, lightly seasoning with salt and
pepper. Transfer to a serving dish and set aside.

3 Return the skillet to medium heatthen add the butter. Sauté the
shallots and garlic until fragrant, about 2 minutes. Add the lemon
zest and the veggie broth, simmering about 5 minutes. Stir in
the heavy cream and 2 tablespoons of the lemon juice, then add the
peas, reserved veggies, and bowties. Add the Parmesan and
the remaining 1 tablespoon lemon juice. Finish by adding the
cherry tomatoes, basil, and more salt and pepper. Let your love
for this spring dish bloom.

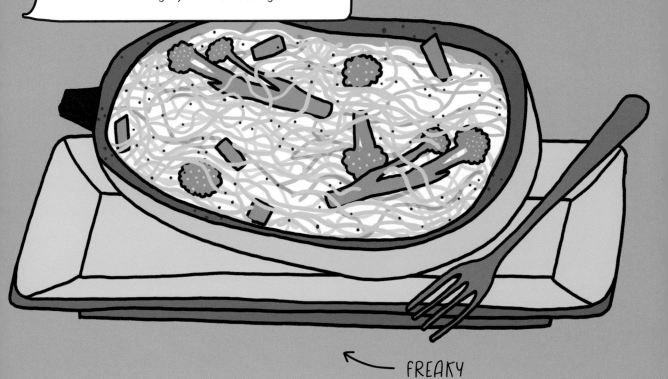

WHO NEEDS FOREPLAY WHEN YOU CAN GO WILD WITH THREE TYPES OF CHEESE? The Sext Me Maybe Squash Lasagna is a piping-hot excuse to eat your veggies, but it's here to mess around. Top this recipe with the Get Some Garlic Breadcrumbs (page 35) and call it your latest fetish, because it feels a little bit naughty but tastes so right.

← — FREAKY

SEXT ME MAYBE
SQUASH "LASAGNA"

1 Preheat the oven to 450°F. Drizzle some water on a microwave-safe dish and place one half of the squash flesh-side down. Cook on high for 10 minutes to steam. Repeat with the second half.

2 In a large skillet, heat the olive oil over medium heat. When the oil is shimmering, sauté the garlic and broccoli until the broccoli brightens, about 3–5 minutes. Remove from the heat and transfer to a large bowl.

3 When the squash is cooked, shred the flesh with a fork and transfer to the bowl with the broccoli. Mix the squash noodles with the mozzarella, Parmesan, Italian seasoning, and salt and pepper. Scoop the mixture back into the squash shells and top with the blue cheese. Place on a baking sheet, and bake on the lower rack for 10 minutes. Move up to the top rack and broil until lightly browned, about 2 minutes. Remove from the oven and indulge in this sizzler.

 SPICE LEVEL

1 spaghetti squash, halved lengthwise and seeded

1 tablespoon extra-virgin olive oil

4 cloves garlic, minced

1 cup broccoli florets

3/4 cup shredded mozzarella

2 tablespoons freshly grated Parmesan

3/4 teaspoon Italian seasoning

Salt and pepper

2 tablespoons crumbled blue cheese

KEEP IT CASUAL CARBONARA

SERVES 2

4 tablespoons butter

2 cloves garlic, chopped

2 cups sweet potato ribbons

1 cup sliced cremini mushrooms

Salt and pepper

2/3 cup half-and-half

1 tablespoon cornstarch

2 cups baby spinach

4 slices cooked bacon, chopped

1/2 cup freshly grated Parmesan

1 In a large skillet, melt the butter over medium-high heat. Sauté the garlic until fragrant, about 1 minute, then add the sweet potato ribbons and mushrooms. Season with salt and pepper and cook for another 3 minutes, stirring occasionally.

2 In a small bowl, whisk together the half-and-half and cornstarch. Slowly pour the mixture into the skillet until the sauce thickens a little. Add the spinach and bacon, then toss together until the spinach is wilted and the flavors meld. Transfer to bowls, top with Parmesan, and canoodle with those noodles.

MIRROR SELFIE LETTUCE WRAPS

1 Cook the rice noodles according to the package instructions. Drain and set aside.

2 In a small bowl, whisk together the soy sauce, fish sauce, brown sugar, sriracha, and water.

3 In a large skillet, heat the avocado oil over medium-high heat. When the oil is shimmering, sauté the garlic, ginger, onion, and ground chicken for about 3–4 minutes until the chicken is cooked through. Reduce the heat and pour in the sauce. Sprinkle in the scallions before removing from the heat.

4 Arrange the lettuce leaves on a serving dish. Evenly distribute the rice noodles, chicken mixture, cucumbers, and Thai basil across the lettuce cups.

 SPICE LEVEL

4 ounces rice noodles

1 tablespoon soy sauce

1 tablespoon fish sauce

1/2 tablespoon dark brown sugar

1/2 tablespoon sriracha

2 tablespoons warm water

1 tablespoon avocado oil

1 clove garlic, minced

1/2 tablespoon minced ginger

1/4 red onion, chopped

1/2 pound ground chicken

1 scallion, thinly sliced

6 bibb lettuce leaves

1/2 small English cucumber, chopped

1/4 cup chopped fresh Thai basil

NOW & FOREVER
TURKEY MEATBALLS

SERVES 2

½ pound ground turkey

½ cup chopped
fresh cilantro

¼ cup shredded
mozzarella

4 cloves garlic, minced

½ teaspoon Italian
seasoning

½ teaspoon red pepper
flakes

Salt and pepper

1½ cups Red Flag Red
Sauce (page 24)

1 tablespoon butter

Juice of ½ lemon

2 medium zucchinis,
spiralized

1 In a large mixing bowl, use your hands to combine the ground
   turkey, cilantro, mozzarella, garlic, Italian seasoning, red pepper
   flakes, salt, and pepper until the seasonings are evenly distributed.
   Form into meatballs and set aside.

2 In a saucepan, heat the red sauce over medium heat to
   warm through.

3 In a large skillet, melt the butter over medium-low heat. Cook
   the meatballs, rotating, until they are brown and cooked through,
   about 6–8 minutes. Spritz with the lemon juice and spoon the
   juices atop the meatballs while they cook. Add the zoodles to
   the same pan and cook until tender-crisp, about 4 minutes.

4 Transfer the zoodles and the meatballs to a serving plate and ladle
   on as much red sauce as you can handle.

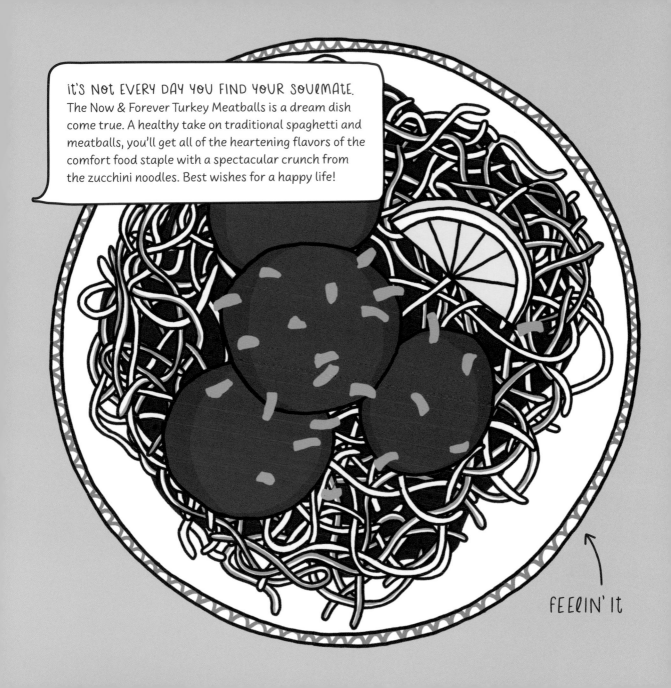

VIBE CHECK VIETNAMESE SALAD

1 In a large bowl, whisk together the lime juice, brown sugar, fish sauce, sesame oil, garlic, and red pepper flakes. Add the spiralized carrot and cucumber and toss to combine. Sprinkle the scallion, cilantro, peanuts, and sesame seeds when serving this hot one.

🔥 **HOT TIP** This noodle salad is hot and cold, not unlike those vibes you're getting. To make it a full meal that satisfies, toss it with cooked shrimp.

SPICE LEVEL

- 1½ tablespoons lime juice
- 2 teaspoons light brown sugar
- ½ tablespoon fish sauce
- 1 teaspoon sesame oil
- 1 clove garlic, minced
- ¼ teaspoon red pepper flakes
- 1 medium carrot, spiralized
- ½ large English cucumber, spiralized
- 1 scallion, sliced
- 2 tablespoons chopped fresh cilantro
- 1 tablespoon chopped unsalted peanuts
- 1 teaspoon black sesame seeds (optional)

THE HOTTIES

5

NOODS
tHAt ARE

F*&#BOY FETTUCCINI

SPICE LEVEL

2 tablespoons
extra-virgin olive oil

1/2 red onion, diced

2 spicy Italian sausage links

1 1/2 cloves garlic,
crushed

1/2 large red chili, diced

1 cup jarred
arrabbiata sauce

1 teaspoon sugar

4 ounces fettuccini noodles

Salt and pepper

Freshly grated Parmesan

1 Cook the fettuccini noodles according to the package instructions. Drain and set aside.

2 In a large saucepan, heat the olive oil over medium heat. When the oil is shimmering, add in the onion and sauté until fragrant, about 1–2 minutes. Remove the sausage from its casing and stir it in, along with the garlic and chili, and cook until lightly browned and glistening.

3 Pour in the arrabbiata sauce. Fill a third of the used measuring cup with water and pour it into the pan. Let the contents of the pan simmer before adding the sugar, and salt and pepper to taste.

4 Stir the cooked fettuccini into the sauce until well combined. Get your F*&#boy Fettuccini on your plate, stat, and sprinkle it with Parmesan.

🔥 HOT TIP Show this recipe a little love by cooking up a half portion of the How You Doin' Homemade Italian Sausage (page 32). Like any f*&#boy, it might be a waste of your time, but you'll think about it long after it's gone.

PREPARE FOR THE SLOW BURN. What looks like a simple bowl of rice noodles is a stunner in disguise. Let the heat between you and the Charm Me Chili Garlic Noodles build until you just can't take it anymore. When you surrender to your last bite, you'll wonder how you missed all the warning signs.

SO SUAVE

CHARM ME
CHILI GARLIC NOODLES

SPICE LEVEL

1 Cook the rice noodles about 1 minute shy of the package instructions. Drain and set aside.

2 In a skillet, heat the avocado oil over medium heat. When the oil is shimmering, sauté the shallots and garlic until fragrant, about 3 minutes. Toss in the ginger and the white parts of the scallion, about 3 minutes more. Stir in the chili garlic sauce, tamari, lime juice, brown sugar, sriracha, and sesame oil and let the flavors meld another 3–5 minutes.

3 Fold in the rice noodles until well coated. Dish it up and sprinkle with the red pepper flakes and cilantro. Get ready for a hot night in.

4 ounces wide rice noodles

1 tablespoon avocado oil

1 shallot, sliced

3 small cloves garlic, minced

1/2 tablespoon minced ginger

1 scallion, sliced

1 tablespoon tamari

11/2 tablespoons chili garlic sauce

1/2 tablespoon lime juice

1/2 tablespoon brown sugar

1/2 tablespoon sriracha

1/2 tablespoon sesame oil

1/2 teaspoon red pepper flakes

2 tablespoons chopped fresh cilantro

SMOKESHOW SHORT RIB PASTA

SERVES 2

11/2 pounds bone-in beef short ribs

Salt and pepper

2 slices bacon

1 medium yellow onion, chopped

3 cloves garlic, minced

1 cup dry red wine

1 (6-ounce) can tomato paste

1/4 teaspoon ground nutmeg

1 bay leaf

1/2 Parmesan rind

4 ounces campanelle noodles

1/4 cup freshly grated Parmesan

2 tablespoons chopped fresh parsley

1 Season the short ribs with salt and pepper. In a skillet, cook the bacon over medium heat until crisp. Remove the bacon and sear the short ribs in the same skillet over medium-high heat, browning each side.

2 Transfer the short ribs to a slow cooker. Chop up the bacon and add it to the slow cooker, followed by the onion, garlic, red wine, tomato paste, nutmeg, bay leaf, and Parmesan rind. Cover and cook on low for 6–8 hours.

3 Cook the campanelle noodles about 1 minute shy of the package instructions. Drain and set aside.

4 Remove the bay leaf and the Parmesan rind from the slow cooker. Shred the short rib meat with forks, discard the bones, and give the sauce a stir. Ladle the sauce over the campanelle noodles, give it your best sprinkle with the Parmesan, and top with parsley.

🔥 **HOT TIP** If you don't have a slow cooker, let this smoke show sizzle on low in a large pot for 3–4 hours, stirring occasionally. Just don't burn your house down. That's too hot.

GOOD IN BED
EGG DROP NOODLE SOUP

SERVES 2

1 Cook the ramen noodles about 1 minute shy of the package instructions. Drain and set aside.

2 In a medium saucepan, heat the grapeseed oil over medium-high heat. When the oil is shimmering, sauté the onion until fragrant and soft, about 5 minutes. Stir in the ginger and garlic and cook for another minute, and then add the crushed tomatoes and veggie broth. Reduce the heat and let simmer for about 15 minutes.

3 In a small bowl, whisk together the eggs and about a teaspoon each of salt and white pepper. Return to the soup and stir in the brown sugar and a pinch of salt, and then bring the soup to a boil. Drizzle in the whisked eggs without stirring, and remove the pot from the heat after a minute.

4 Dish out the noodles and soup into bowls and top with chili oil if you want it hot and heavy.

 SPICE LEVEL

1 (3-ounce) package ramen noodles

1 tablespoon grapeseed oil

1/2 small yellow onion, chopped

2 teaspoons minced ginger

1 clove garlic, minced

1 (14-ounce) can crushed tomatoes

2 cups Steamy Stare Veggie Broth (page 20)

2 eggs

Salt and white pepper

1 tablespoon brown sugar

1 tablespoon chili oil

SLIDE INTO MY DMs
STROZZAPRETI

4 ounces strozzapreti or short noodles

2 tablespoons extra-virgin olive oil

1/2 pound How You Doin' Homemade Italian Sausage (page 32)

1 large clove garlic, minced

1 bunch broccolini, coarsely chopped

1/4 teaspoon red pepper flakes

Salt and pepper

Freshly grated Parmesan

1 Cook the strozzapreti noodles about 1 minute shy of the package instructions. Drain, reserving 1/2 cup pasta water, and set aside.

2 In a frying pan, heat the olive oil over medium heat. Break up and brown the sausage in the pan for 5–7 minutes. Remove the sausage from the pan and brown the garlic in the sausage fat. Toss in the broccolini and sauté until it's bright green. Return the sausage to the pan and add the noodles, red pepper flakes, and the reserved pasta water. Stir until the ingredients look glossy.

3 Dish out a heartwarming helping and sprinkle the Parmesan to finish.

TURN ON THOSE NOTIFICATIONS, THIS IS ONE SPICY SURPRISE YOU'LL WANT TO SEE AGAIN AND AGAIN. Slide into My DMs Strozzapreti is anything but complicated: a quick sauté of bitter-but-in-a-good-way broccolini, spicy Italian sausage that's just your type, and a kick of red pepper flakes makes this an easier path to epicurean pleasure than if it had popped up unsolicited.

FEELIN' SPICY

DREAMBOAT ARRABIATA

1 Cook the gemelli noodles about 1 minute shy of the package instructions. Drain and set aside.

2 In a large skillet, heat the olive oil over medium heat. When the oil is shimmering, sauté the garlic and red pepper flakes until fragrant, about 1 minute. Add the shrimp and sauté until they are lightly browned on each side, but not curled tight. Stir in the red sauce and bring to a gentle boil. Reduce the heat, fold in the gemelli noodles, and season with salt and pepper.

3 Get this fiery feast into bowls with a ton of Parmesan and a sprinkle of parsley.

🔥 **HOT TIP** If you don't have time for the Red Flag Red Sauce and just want a quick-and-dirty version, use a jar of the store-bought stuff or a can of crushed tomatoes.

 SPICE LEVEL

4 ounces gemelli noodles

1 tablespoon extra-virgin olive oil

1 clove garlic, crushed

1–2 tablespoons red pepper flakes

1/2 pound shrimp, peeled and deveined

1 1/2 cups Red Flag Red Sauce (page 24)

Salt and pepper

1/4 cup freshly grated Parmesan

1 tablespoon chopped fresh parsley

SWEETHEART
SAUSAGE & SPAGHETTI

- 4 ounces spaghetti noodles
- 2 tablespoons extra-virgin olive oil
- 2 spicy Italian sausage links, diced
- 1 cup cherry tomatoes
- 1 clove garlic, thinly sliced
- 1/4 cup grated Pecorino
- 1 teaspoon red pepper flakes
- 4–5 fresh basil leaves, torn

1 Cook the spaghetti noodles about 1 minute shy of the package instructions. Drain, reserving 1 cup of the pasta water, and set aside.

2 In a large skillet, heat the olive oil over medium heat. When the oil is shimmering, sauté the sausage, browning on each side, about 5 minutes. Remove the sausage and add the cherry tomatoes to the same skillet. When they begin to burst, stir in the garlic and cook until fragrant, about 2 minutes. Return the sausage to the pan, add the spaghetti, and pour in the pasta water. Toss the contents together for another minute.

3 Dress this bad boy up in Pecorino, red pepper flakes, and basil before admiring your work.

ADIOS, CUFFING SEASON, HELLO HOT GIRL SUMMER PESTO PASTA. Tell the expectations of the sweatiest season to kick rocks, and instead break out flavors that have all the signs of a summer tryst without any of the hassle. With fresh veggies, even fresher pesto, and some serious jalapeño heat, this fettuccini is a ten.

BEAUTY

HOT GIRL SUMMER PESTO PASTA

1 Cook the fettuccini noodles about 1 minute shy of the package instructions. Drain and set aside.

2 In a large skillet, heat the olive oil over medium heat. Melt the butter, and sauté the zucchini, corn, and shallots until the veggies brighten, about 5 minutes. Season with salt and pepper.

3 Toss in the fettuccini noodles, lemon juice, pesto and jalapeños. Stir to combine, and then dish out this hot dish.

 SPICE LEVEL

4 ounces fettuccini noodles

1 tablespoon extra-virgin olive oil

1 tablespoon butter

1 small zucchini, chopped

1 cup corn kernels

1 shallot, chopped

Salt and pepper

Juice of 1/2 lemon

2 tablespoons Looking Fresh Pesto (page 28)

1/2 jalapeño, seeded and minced

HIT IT & QUIT IT
PAN-FRIED NOODLES

SPICE LEVEL

4 ounces Hong Kong egg noodles

2½ tablespoons peanut oil

3 tablespoons soy sauce

2 teaspoons rice wine

1 teaspoon sesame oil

1 cup thinly sliced scallions

1 tablespoon minced ginger

5 cloves garlic, thinly sliced

2 eggs, beaten

½ cup edamame

½ cup sliced shiitake mushrooms

1–2 teaspoon sriracha

Juice of ½ lime

1 Cook the egg noodles about 2 minutes shy of the package instructions. Drain, toss with ½ tablespoon of the peanut oil, and lay them out on a baking sheet.

2 In a small bowl, whisk together the soy sauce, rice wine, and sesame oil. Stir in the scallions and ginger.

3 In a large skillet, heat 2 tablespoons of the peanut oil over medium-high heat. When the oil is shimmering, sauté the garlic until fragrant, about 2 minutes. Pour in half of the sauce and cook, stirring about 1 minute. Add the noodles and toss in the pan before adding the eggs, edamame, mushrooms, and the rest of the sauce. Stir-fry for about 2 minutes, or until the eggs are cooked. Remove from the heat, drizzle with sriracha, spritz with the lime juice, and serve this hottie up.

LOVE AT FIRST SWIPE
PISTACHIO RIGATONI

SERVES 2

1 Cook the rigatoni noodles about 1 minute shy of the package instructions. Drain and set aside.

2 In a large skillet, heat the olive oil over medium heat. When the oil is shimmering, sauté the shallots, garlic, and red pepper flakes until fragrant, about 3 minutes. Pour in the chicken broth and bring to a boil. Fold in the spinach and season with allspice. Toss in the rigatoni noodles, preserved lemon, and lemon juice.

3 Get this citrus stunner in front of you and garnish with the pistachios and Pecorino.

🔥 **HOT TIP** If you are getting after this recipe using the Check You Out Chicken Broth, you can probably ease up on the lemon juice since the broth is already quite lemony. If using regular chicken or veggie broth, stick to what's listed.

 SPICE LEVEL

4 ounces rigatoni noodles

2 tablespoons extra-virgin olive oil

1 large shallot, finely chopped

2 cloves garlic, thinly sliced

1 teaspoon red pepper flakes

1 cup Check You Out Chicken Broth (page 16)

1 (5-ounce) bag fresh spinach, chopped

1 teaspoon ground allspice

2 tablespoons diced preserved lemon

1 tablespoon lemon juice

¼ cup chopped pistachios

2 tablespoons grated Pecorino

INDEX